Gallery Books
Editor: Peter Fallon

THE MORNING TRAIN

Gerald Dawe

THE
MORNING
TRAIN

Gallery Books

U.S. DISTRIBUTOR
DUFOUR EDITIONS
CHESTER SPRINGS
PA 19425-0007
(610) 458-5005

The Morning Train
is first published
simultaneously in paperback
and in a clothbound edition
on 11 November 1999.

The Gallery Press
Loughcrew
Oldcastle
County Meath
Ireland

ISBN 1 85235 259 0 (*paperback*)
 1 85235 260 4 (*clothbound*)

The Gallery Press acknowledges the financial assistance
of An Chomhairle Ealaíon / The Arts Council, Ireland,
and the Arts Council of Northern Ireland.

Contents

for Dorothea

PART ONE

'One is in a country that is no longer here and not quite there.'

— F. Scott Fitzgerald

The Minos Hotel

1

There's always a guy in the pool
throwing a ball to somebody
who never catches and they're bound
to be German, braceleted, bronzed,

already with their place set out
under the sun. Whereas an English
couple's just paid a visit for
the kiddies' sake and grows more

adventurous with each passing day.
Before dinner I survey the bay —
Greeks on their evening stroll
talk up close and ignore us all.

2

Hungover from the local wine,
I'm sitting out on the balcony
of our white hotel room;
tourists walk about below me —

mats, bum-bags, li-los, sun-hats,
visors — and the sea's chopping up.
At the little Oratory, some people
stand looking far away.

The hills are smoking; a plane
descends. A yacht skiffs by
like a butterfly.
What'll we do for lunch?

3

I'm not drowning, I'm waving
at all you folks out there
in the rising tide. *Confrères*
of the western world: potbellied,

many-childrened, thin as rakes,
your heads bob in ones and twos
or else you make a circle
and swim into the Mediterranean.

He looks like Picasso, she a goddess.
Water spills down breasts and flanks
to where you raise a mighty arm,
bowling water, like a water-wheel.

4

The widow-women dressed in black
appear along the seashore by
their son's Skoda or Toyota van.
They carry infants, bags of fruit.

They do not travel. One daughter
is in Melbourne, Australia;
another's in Toronto, Canada.
And the women who live in villages

among the ochre hills,
in serried streets, take their time.
I have seen them, too, at home,
wearing coats of grey and blue.

5

And that time on the balcony
it was boiling rain,
and from the valley the odd shout,
the *pleet-pleet* of some bird

or other. Bats swerved about
and, mistaken for stars,
satellites screened back to base
the movement of armies and the like

while in the half-light fireflies
popped and toady snakes played
blithely among the village bins.
It was a heaven of sorts.

6

So say your body is a cello —
in the moonlit airless room
the sea heaves to under
(are they?) eucalyptus trees

and the little fishing boats;
the squawking cats —
you'd need a Modigliani
to get it right:

hip to hip, the sheet
light as a feather
and you, lying on the left side,
adrift in the full-length mirror.

7

Even at this time of day —
six or seven — cars speed by
the trumpeting siren of an ambulance
on the Place de la Madeleine.

You breathe in rhythm
with all that goes on outside.
Cranes swivel over the tops
of these apartment blocks;

the ritzy restaurants will soon
have tables and chairs set out.
I reach over to fix the duvet.
What year is this? Which century?

8

And, to cap it all,
a weekend in the Metropole!
The very thing.
Mr Magritte peeps out from behind

his newspaper; the dainty dogs
stretch themselves momentarily
and we order another.
The SS are polishing their boots

in the rooms overhead. Imagine
the nightly curfew, the daily raid.
And in a fountain of leafy rain
sparrows play to our delight.

9

Why the people in the hotel ad
look as if they'll vaporise
like the crew of *Star Trek* —
who can tell?

I can't read the writing on the wall.
What sounds Russian is really Portuguese.
Crawling his way up through
the tourist shops and naff boutiques

a man, medieval and grotesque,
begs for alms.
He parts the waters.
We look the other way.

10

There is always 'somewhere'.
Like the Navigators who saw
the blue glass of the ocean
and decided to go beyond

the mountainous cloud-banks.
From our own spot here
atop the Auto-Estrado
a luxury liner swans past

factoryship and frigate;
windsurfers, our vibrant souls,
nip and tuck above the waves;
the first sighting of land is like the last.

PART TWO

'By day the frolic, and the dance by night.'
— Samuel Johnson

Black Dog

In the house next door the newly-born baby
gurgles and cries for mother;

in the one on up, a bowl of flowers
bristles in the bay window.

That poor old heavy-footed black dog
has been let out and barks to get back in again.

On some of the terrace the original double-doors
stand alone — painted green; frosted glass.

Your head lifts off the pillow and asks,
What was that? Never mind, says

the blocked-up chimney, the grey attic,
and silent yard, never mind.

Ascension Thursday

He climbs the wall and then,
like a tight-rope walker, sidles along.

For all the world, this man,
who turns metalwork for a living,

could be unattached to anything
and is merely up there —

among the security lights and gutters,
the bathroom windows and rogue flowers —

having taken off for himself.
When the electronic church-bells gong,

he doesn't flinch from the job at hand.
On the contrary, he simply disappears.

Resolution and Independence

The girls are at their radiant screens,
columns of figures that put them
in touch with the world — Zurich,
Hong Kong, New York, and Mulgrave Street.

❖

Qualm at Waterstone's:
Hold on, she said,
I'll put you through to Biography
and they'll look for you there.

❖

These things are sent to try us
went through my head
as the street rose to meet me
and I just made Moon's Corner.

❖

There should always be
THE IRISH YEAST CO.
shining in the twilight
of College Street.

Note on the Text

From the very beginning — laid up,
with the other shouts of kids,
the milk-float hum, and the mandatory dog —

he settled for an eyeful of daylight,
brief looks, a woman singing in snatches,
the ghostly body spotted in a bedroom,

the plot and gable of introspective gardens,
the window's acreage of hillside,
the original silence; the slacked fire.

The Visible World

Troubles

Saturday morning — the bit that's left over
  from the night before, and there are still a few knocking
    about.
In a while, the first bus and all those who work
  a six-day-week will shut doors on their man or woman,
the kids, monk's bench, ascending stairs, and they will hear,
  or think they hear, a voice crying about love, troubled
    love,
even at this time of day.

1958

It was in the waiting room where trolley-buses merged
with the stink of a pub just opened that I looked out
  to the overgrown cemetery with tombs lodged in its walls.
I remember the queue of men, cheeks flushed by racking
    coughs,
  women with children who talked under bated breath,
    cardigans
over their good blouses, the nylon cuffing on a high-heel
  shoe.

The Break-Up

Riding up front in the Removals van was like being in the
   Army tank
I was lifted into one Open Day — our furniture stacked
   in the back. I was so high up I didn't notice the knocks
as we took this blind corner and that bad bend, so when we
   finally arrived and the light poured in the barn-like doors
I half-expected birds to come tearing out of the tables
   and teapots like screaming bats.

Charades

His grandmother's sister's daughter is over
   and in the front room with the adults —
      the sofa pushed back, trays with drinks,
the fire burning brightly, peals of laughter — the boy finally
   steps forward:
      'A song. Three words. Beginning with . . .'
and it goes on for ages until a voice inside hisses, *Show-off.*

The Grove

The park railings were bent just enough so you could get
    your
head through, then the rest. Like slipping a noose.
    The same feeling as walking up the gangway whose
    wooden slats
showed a foot of water down between the ship and quay
    side.
    Or like the beautiful girl in the circus who fell from the
    highwire
and is falling still — a sycamore seed spinning away out of
    control
to almost reach the blue, untouchable blue, of the lough.

Illuminations

When I saw the man with an inflatable globe of the world
    carrying it like a football I immediately thought about
the Geography room at Orangefield. We were watching a
    film
on Alaskan oil, or it could have been Peruvian Indians —
bears fishing, gold *ingots* — and the dumb backs of our
    heads
lit from within the same beam of dusty light.

Glad Eyes

In the necessary room of cubicles and mirrors I am absent-
  minded, hear only the cistern fill, the automatic hand-
    drier
go off and on, and I stare at the patent invincible,
  Armitage Shanks, while in the wings stand other shadows —
Aunt Annie's puffed face smelling of peppermint,
  the girl on the Downview bus crossing her legs
though our glad eyes never let on, *our glad eyes never let on.*

Voodoo Child

Cocktail sticks all over the place — their severe heads
and brittle bodies scattered after the Hen's Night;
  exhausted souls, wandering about my attic bedroom,
are looking for each other, in black-and-white.

Earth Sign

I slept for ages, or so I thought.
One of those great afternoons, the child out for the count,
  and your mother pottered about.
I was flat on the cropped grass watching the smallest signs
  of life on the planet and the sky in the window
going the wrong way. I held on tight.

Oxfords

The click of the steel-tip of Mr Lemon's *Oxfords*
drew my attention one night as I was looking out,
the avenue quiet, all right, give or take a car.
Wherever the trouble is it's not here.
His regimental navy blazer's silver buttons
like little moons, with double-front and cuffs;
even his jet-black hair gleams in the night.

And the man doing the floor
in the Deramore went down but came back up again
in the famous torpedo'd DESTROYER,
what do you call its name —
or was he the merchant seaman?
Anyway he's gone now, as have
the two on either side of us —
one was a clerk high-up in the Post Office,
the other a lonely spinster we knew nothing about.

And the old fellas are gaping out of their front rooms
at what's going on
but does it all matter anymore, I ask myself,
does it ever?

Quartz

for Katrina Goldstone

So there is something I want to know,
great-grandmother, reclining on whichever
foreign shore or ambrosial meadow,
taking a second look at the old place —

the valiant village, the provincial district,
the back-breaking hill-climb to the apartment,
the quiet evening square in this country town
or that frontier post, down by the coastal resort

of some famous lake, say, with Roman baths,
or a minority language — I want to know
who your grand dame was, or paterfamilias,
disembarking in a draughty shed, thinking

Liverpool or Belfast was really New York,
blinking in the greyish light of a noisy dawn,
looking out for rooming houses, a decent hotel,
putting one foot in front of the other,

taking the first right and walking, walking,
past the shipping offices and custom houses,
the rattling trams and carters and mill girls,
the steep factories and squat churches till the hills

converge upon this three-storied terrace
with the curtains drawn, the bell-pull shining,
and you pull the bell-pull and in whatever
English you'd learned you stepped in.

Europa

Kristallnacht, 1938

Observe the distracted faces of these men
who are Jews, attempting to march and look casual.
See, too, the shoddy uprighteousness
of those who are leading this forced march,

but do not miss the woman's shy smile
and the three men under the trees
who look in different directions all at once.
This shot is seen through the eyes of a smiling woman.

'90s Idyll

From the unscathed London sky
a gull reconnoîtres those sleeping rough;
joggers in shell-suits and woolly gloves;
the deep-water wharf and fuel dump

that once were the docks. Phones ring
non-stop and security cameras scan
the clearway, underpass, the landscaped roads.
The bus comes and goes without a soul on board.

Hero at Lansdowne

The thugs we watch and love to hate
have left the island.
In this particular photograph I've kept
the skin-headed patriot

looks as if he's singing in an opera.
Behind all is chaos
and we are appropriately shocked
at such hellish behaviour.

This crazy, shorn bloke, his bomber-
jacket half-off, screams
at the unseen gods way above him
and below: *Fuckin' bastards. Scum.*

Anon

My Prague scarf has no name nor maker.
I bought it that time we waltzed around
the freezing city: trad jazz in the bars,
the foggy castle above, shadowy beggars

on the bridge and the foreign kids
hanging loose on the corporate squares.
This was hip, my dream city, you were it,
and no one could see me in behind
the Prague scarf, hidden like a bandit.

The Old Jewish Cemetery, Lodz

Tabernacle, opened book, theatrum,
dove, headstones topsy-turvy,
till six unfilled pits
take back from the atrocious silence
the caretaker's sleeping dog,
the nondescript side door of exit.

Resting

after Chagall

This is not a prayer although the man's in a state
somewhere between sleep and supplication.
The fir-tree has borne the brunt of the wind
but the sow and horse are unheeding.
    Does he dream or is something at his throat?
The faint pressure of scarlet night draws close
and he, who is really as much you as he is me,
expects the worst that this time and place can offer.
Or else there is something quite different going on.
    Such things are left with the man lying down, and resting.

In Memory of James Joyce

Just thought I'd drop you a line
given the fact that I happened to be walking
the same streets as you once did.
It was, of course, raining,

and down by Nuns' Island the houses faded
to a faint pointillist light.
At the derelict mill up-for-sale,
schoolgirls in greys and blacks

sped past with U2 badges on racing-bikes.
They'll keep going till they are far
from Rahoon, Wellpark and Castlelawn.
The pity is, would it have been any

different if they had known about
your woman, Nora, or how you both managed
moving from flat to flat
and put their country on the map

of a mostly indifferent universe?
Heading into town, the Curragh Line
is like the road in *The Great Gatsby*
except the billboard here is the dump.

Every house is an El Dorado
while an ancient tower teeters on the brink.
So much for the past. We must make
our own choices and live with them —

immaculate blinds and ornamental brasses —
as the Corrib seeps into glinting lakes.
What would you think of the new estates
hugging either shore, or the Telecom mast

picking up our fervent calls across the water
to a son that's gone, or a daughter?
I tip my hat as you pass by,
a preoccupied man in shabby gutties.

Bloomsday, Galway 1987

The Night's Takings

for Cathal McCabe

The whores had disappeared by the time
we got there and the barman smiled,
totting up the night's takings.
So here we were, two Northern lads perched
on high stools in the middle of Europe,

the last snow black on the cobblestones,
a way down marble stairs to the seen-
it-all-before janitor, the ballroom kitted
out for ex-party types, the local mafia,
as we looked along the longest street —

the shoplights dimmed, the watchful mannequins,
the clackety-clack of the military,
the wary taxi, the metallic sky,
and the inevitable echo
that is neither here nor there.

Last Words

Hatted William Burroughs is gone.
In *The New Yorker* he wrote:
'No nothing. There in the pitiless
noon streets. No letters.'

When I met him he was like a deathly
clerk of works — cold and disgusted.
Was it the same thing as Leopardi's poem
to himself: the world mud; better off dead?

A Dream of Magritte

for Hugh and Anne Logue

All I could see when I looked in
was the builder's gear — ladders,
trestles, laths of wood, concrete mix,
putty — that kind of thing.

Shrubs pressed against the far window;
a door half-opened to a hall
where I fancied he was loitering,
trying hard not to be seen.

A wisp of smoke curls into a question —
the profile of a man in a bowler hat
flies up into the blue-and-white sky —
But what am I really looking at, what?

rue Esseghem, Brussels

Promises

To wake like this in the middle of the night
and hear a bird, I'm not sure which,
in solo run, then pad down to the kitchen
and notice the blue light of the moon
give way to the dawn is OK too.

❖

In private gardens and apartment blocks
they are already up and showered.
From Valhalla, Greenfields, Haven,
the gates remain open; gravel
spits out from under the twisted wheel.

❖

That flash of thigh at the downstairs
front window when I get into the car —
her hair bells and she has a quick look
at what kind of day it promises to be.

❖

A chilly light takes hold of clothes,
lotions, little bottles of perfume.
By chance, too, there's a necklace hanging there.

Vertigo

I pace behind you both and feel
the earth's steady incline
so that when you keep walking,
higher and higher, I want to sit
with my back square against
the flipped horizon; the rip-tide.

❖

Alongside the foreshore I take from the sea
muskets, boxes of butter, timber for housebuilding,
a lopsided mine and shark's fin; vestments,
and the last landlord's swollen ledgers.

Questions of Geography

The morning train you call the Express
stops along the way. Why is it, as we
sit there talking, I see a young woman's face
in the underground hurtling to work
so that by the time we've reached Blackrock
it's like we are starting all over again —
a fair wind to our backs; the sea calm?

❖

When I go on top, or you do,
and we play like swing-boats,
back and forth, back and forth,
where is it that we go to, what land mass,
when I go on top or vice versa?

❖

Up here, next the chimney and solitary gull,
I reckon I can see you too, wherever.

In Ron's Place

I was sitting up in Ron's place
among the mountains,
church bells followed by church bells,
then 'April in Paris',

when I realised that a person
can only take so much in.
I'd been lying in my cot
for the guts of a week —

Hong Kong or Singapore flu —
and could hardly lift my head for you,
lover, lady, wife.
I thought this was it —

the end, to simply waste away,
neutral and inert,
without a bit taken,
the brassy taste of stomach juices,

swollen glands, blocked passageways,
the shivers, energy levels
at an all-time low
when, as I say,

I was listening to Bird, 'April in Paris',
the church bells went counting,
then the tower up here
in the silent hills,

where the only sound
is the postman's moped,
a couple of voices under the window,
before you really see

the mountains beneath us
and the brazen light of day
cover all things, great and small —
lizards slipping in and out

of the warming roof tiles,
the logs dissembling into cobwebs
and dust, the table and chair
moved to where you take the sun . . .

And I fall back to sleep,
this time in a couchette,
listening to the wheels brace and tack
to miles and miles of railway track.

At one station —
its long name in black and white,
the row of lorries parked in
a yellowish light from the waiting room —

the deadpan voice announces
where we are and where we are going next
as we arrive and depart
the all-night factories, the cubist blocks

of flats, the shapes of installations
in the darkness, snowy embankments,
sidings, cranes, sheds,
and then nothing again.

In the mountains, there you feel free.
I read much of the night
and go south in the winter,
the wheels at my head, the door double-locked.

The countryside flees
and I wake with a jolt.
Are you still there?
Is the sun still out?

Travels

for Mark Mulreany

In our Greek part of the garden
the head of Zeus nods away;
the dried stems of sunflowers hang
their weeping Christ-like faces;

the fallen copper leaves,
the Cretan frescoes,
the sails of bed-linen,
the lantern of bird food;

the seashore rhododendrons,
the waving bougainvillaea,
the coiling cable of the night-light,
a fleet of spiders and ants;

and the mascara'd finch
dancing along the flowering wall.

Summer Journal

for Brendan Kennelly

Through the porthole of a window
    the blue muggy night is perforated
with the sound of foghorns.
    Dogs answer each other back
and then it thunders again with spectacular effect.
    The girls are sleeping in the cool apartment;
shadows like planes cast over the lawn.
    I'm in two minds between *Tender is the Night*
and the TV's mute hectic images
    which flash worldwide the breaking news
of a hillside trek and scorched villages,
    the bedecked impromptu briefing.

❖

The ignominious beetle covers oceans of sand
    but the man or woman who drifts
into the sky, paragliding over our prone bodies —
    family groups setting up makeshift home,
couples in their prime and past their prime,
    the odd one alone stretched under the sun
where all are vulnerable, torn this way
    and that, naked, flat, in repose from
the everyday, at sixes and sevens —
    is trussed and hooked to the speeding boat
and, cradled like a baby, looks down
    upon us all with far-seeing love and pity.

❖

Palm doves and swallows in the apricot
    and oleander, the cacophony
of high season; poolside, *Mitteleuropa*
    tans and in silence observes a galleon
take up the full of the Bay.
    The *rosé* goes down like mother's milk;
it's near ninety, best head for cover;
    in the shade local dance music
beats through the scratchy airwaves
    to you on whichever island you stand:
        '*Let us dream it now,*
        And pray for a possible land.'

Human Wishes

Gulls have the best of both worlds here —
the last remaining trawlers ditch
the unsaleable back into the sea
and, when they're not out, skips are gone through.

Families unsure what to do for the day
walk about or stand along the east pier
convinced that all is well, pointing at Howth
to queries about what's over there.

The ferry crosses to the North Wall
but is it really moving? We brace ourselves
against this gusting wind and hail.
The DART shuttles under bridges like a toy train.

Ladies and gentlemen of the People's Park,
hooded lads beyond in the bus shelter,
those well-to-do and those who barely
keep their heads above water —

do we live our lives in vain?
A dog checks along the cold sea-front;
old married couples get on with it.
This is a homecoming of sorts.

Scuba divers at the Forty Foot
bob and duck like seals
caught in the drifting nets.
The coast is clear. Wales

and England ride on the tide;
the sky is laced with jet trails.
By the time we reach the Baths
the aquamarine has turned ice-blue.

'Dear God, such a shocking murder.
How was he ever allowed out?
We're off to France this year. And you?'
And you? And you? And you?

Our selves dissolve into sidestreets,
arm-in-arm, ever so lightly, we go
past the buggy that's been left behind —
the supermarket trolley, the beer-kegs,

the fast-food cartons, the pavements
and kerbstones rooted up by trees,
the white carrier bag snagged in the breeze;
the artisans' cottages, the old lady's open door,

the turn-of-the-century family grocer —
we bring back in with us the brash air
as the gasmen's barrels take off down the street,
the wind bends back our strange mimosa tree

and smashes against these paper-thin windows.
Sun-burst is the breaking cloud-cover upstairs.

❖

Myself and the shoemaker have curtains pulled,
not quite enough, so you can see what
movement there is, inside and out.
He, too, has the radio on, I don't doubt.

A squashed cider-flagon rattles around
the back-lane, the sky races overhead
and the churlish sea explodes;
we contain ourselves as best we can:

the green light of the deep freeze,
the microwave's skinny digits,
the mobile phone on its life-line,
the alarm panel keyed in, the cat's eye

dashboard of the answering machine
and whoever's voice is leaving word.

Acknowledgements

Acknowledgements are due to the editors of *College Green, Fortnight, The Honest Ulsterman, Icarus, The Independent* (London), *The Irish Times, Irish University Review, London Magazine, New Hibernia Review, New Orleans Review, Or Volge L'Anno: At the Year's Turning,* (edited by Marco Sonzogni), *Poetry in Motion, Poetry Ireland Review, Princeton University Library Chronicle, The Recorder* (NY), *Signals* (edited by Adrian Rice), *The Southern Review* (Louisiana), *Verse, The Waterstone's Guide to Irish Books* (edited by Cormac Kinsella) and *The Whoseday Book* where versions of these poems first appeared.

Special thanks to Louise Kidney, Ron Ewart and Toni O'Brien Johnson. The author wishes to acknowledge a Ledig-Rowohlt Fondation Award at Le Chateau de Lavigny, Switzerland.

Note
Minos, a son of Zeus and Europa, was Lord of Crete. After his death he became judge of the Underworld.